The Holy Spirit & The Baptism Of The Holy Spirit

The Holy Spirit & The Baptism Of The Holy Spirit

Sandra Lott

Your New Life Ministries LLC

Contents

Introduction

Thank you for your interest in growing deeper in your knowledge of the Holy Spirit.

The full purpose of the Holy Spirit is to glorify Jesus Christ, guiding, correcting, and comforting us. The Holy Spirit intercedes for us. He also draws you to Jesus, for no one comes to the Father unless he is drawn. We are to be the voice, the hands, and feet for which the Holy Spirit shines through from us to others. We are not to just go to Church and say, "We are a Christian," we are to live it. Living out your daily life as a true child of God-loving people, as a way of life, is the best testimony you will ever have.

Allow the Holy Spirit to teach, and guide you. As you read through this study ask the Lord to speak to your heart and to give you understanding. He will awaken your heart and your mind to the many wonders and gifts of the Holy Spirit. You will grow even closer to God.

Everyone is given the fruit of the Holy Spirit upon receiving Jesus into their heart, but God does not stop there. You are also given gifts, gifts for kingdom purposes. "For we are His workmanship, created in Christ Jesus for good works, which God prepared beforehand that we should walk in them." (Ephesians 2:10)

This book will teach you about being baptized in the Holy Spirit and all the gifts of the Spirit. It will teach you what they are, what they mean, and what they are used for.

As you grow deeper in knowledge of the things of God you will truly be changed and you will shine as a "City on a Hill."

1

Who Is The Holy Spirit

Who is the Holy Spirit?

The Holy Spirit is God, the third person of the Trinity: the Father, Son, and Holy Spirit.

"Therefore go and make disciples of all nations, baptizing them in the name of the Father and of the Son and of the Holy Spirit." Matthew 28:19

The Trinity has always been, since the beginning.

"Then God said, 'Let us make man in Our image, in Our likeness, and let them rule over the fish of the sea and the birds of the air, over the livestock, over all the creatures that move along the ground." Genesis 1:26

The Spirit is from God.

"For who among men knows the thoughts of a man except the man's spirit within him? In the same way, no one knows the thoughts of God except the Spirit of God. We have not received the spirit of the world but the Spirit

who is from God, that we may understand what God has freely given us."
I Corinthians 2:11-12

The Holy Spirit glorifies Jesus, for it is through the sacrificial blood of Christ that we are saved.

"But when He, the Spirit of Truth, comes, He will guide you into all truth. He will not speak on His own; He will speak only what He hears, and He will tell you what is yet to come. He will bring glory to Me by taking from what is Mine and making it known to you. All that belongs to the Father is Mine. That is why I said the Spirit will take from what is Mine and make it known to you." John 16:13-15

The Holy Spirit lives in believers when they are "born again," saved.

"The world cannot accept Him, because it neither sees Him nor knows Him, for He lives with you and will be in you." John 14:17

This is when you ask the Lord Jesus to come into your heart. You are filled with His Holy Spirit at this time. Jesus and the Holy Spirit are both of God. When you ask for the baptism of the Holy Spirit you are totally wrapped up in and filled to the uttermost with the Holy Spirit and the Holy Spirit comes upon you like a cloak.

"But you will receive power when the Holy Spirit comes on you." Acts 1:8

It is like a cup with water in it is the born-again believer with the Spirit in him, as the cup is immersed completely under water is the born-again believer baptized in the Spirit.

2

❧

Understanding The Holy Spirit

To understand the role of the Holy Spirit and the baptism of the Holy Spirit, you must understand the full purpose of Jesus leaving His Holy Spirit with us.

Our carnal nature within us is at war with the spirit and because of that, there is no way that we could ever live up to the Ten Commandments.

"I put this in human terms because you are weak in your natural selves. But now that you have been set free from sin and have become slaves to God, the benefit you reap leads to holiness, and the result is eternal life. For the wages of sin is death, but the gift of God is eternal life in Christ Jesus our Lord." Romans 6:19 / 22-23

The whole purpose of the law was to draw us to God by helping us to see that keeping the law in our own effort is just too difficult.

"Therefore no one will be declared righteous in his sight by observing the law; rather, through the law we become conscious of sin." Romans 3:20

Our Heavenly Father knew that on our own, we could never keep from breaking the law. It was His intention all along in giving the Commandments to help us see what sin is and then sending Jesus to save us from our sins.

"For we know that our old self was crucified with Him so that the body of sin might be done away with, that we should no longer be slaves to sin—because anyone who has died has been freed from sin......For sin shall not be your master, because you are not under law, but under grace." Romans 6:6-7 & 14.

Sin came into the world through Satan and human weakness; salvation came from God's overwhelming love for mankind. Sin keeps us bound, but the love and grace of God frees us from the bondage that living a life of sin will keep you in; it is a life lived as though you were in chains.

"But now, by dying to what once bound us, we have been released from the law so that we serve in the new way of the Spirit, and not in the old way of the written code." Romans 7:6

When hell broke loose, heaven came down and His name is Jesus. Jesus came to draw us to God and He left His Spirit with us to do that, bringing all glory and honor to Jesus. Another purpose of the Holy Spirit is to draw others to Christ through us. As you read through this study you will understand this through the Scriptures God has given in His Holy Word.

"If you love Me, you will obey what I command. And I will ask the Father, and He will give you another Counselor to be with you forever--the Spirit of truth. The world cannot accept Him, because it neither sees Him nor knows Him, for He lives with you and will be in you." John 14:15-17

God loved us so much that He wanted to give us all that we would need to enable us to live a holy life here on earth, and then be able to spend eternity with Him in heaven.

"All this I have spoken while still with you. But the Counselor, the Holy Spirit, whom the Father will send in My name, will remind you of everything I have said to you." John 14:25-26

He not only sent Jesus to be the atonement for our sins, but upon His resurrection into heaven, His Holy Spirit was then made possible to be sent into every heart of every person who received Jesus Christ.

"God made him who had no sin to be sin for us so that in Him we might become the righteousness of God." II Corinthians 5:21

The Holy Spirit reveals and enlightens us to the truths of God. This helps us to understand His Word and His will for our lives.

"No eye has seen, no ear has heard, no mind has conceived what God has prepared for those who love Him but God has revealed it to us by His Spirit." I Corinthians 2:9-10

Upon receiving Jesus Christ into your hearts and forgiveness of your sins; the next step is to be baptized.

"Repent and be baptized, every one of you, in the name of Jesus Christ for the forgiveness of your sins. And you will receive the gift of the Holy Spirit." Acts 2:38

This is an outward showing that you believe and accept Jesus Christ as your personal Lord and Savior.

"In it, only a few people were saved through water, and this water symbolizes baptism that now saves you also--not the removal of dirt from the body but the pledge of a good conscience toward God. It saves you by

the resurrection of Jesus Christ, who has gone into heaven and is at God's right hand--with angels, authorities, and powers in submission to Him." I Peter 3:20-22

We are also called to be baptized by the example that Jesus, Himself set for us.

"I have set you an example that you should do as I have done for you. I tell you the truth, no servant is greater than his master, nor is a messenger greater than the one who sent him. Now that you know these things, you will be blessed if you do them." John 13:15-17

The Lord sent the Holy Spirit to convict the world of sin and also to convict Christians in their everyday lives when they fall, and sin against the Lord.

"Unless I go away, the Counselor will not come to you; but if I go, I will send Him to you. When He comes, He will convict the world of guilt in regard to sin and righteousness and judgment." John 16:7-8

It is Jesus Christ Himself, who baptizes you with the Holy Spirit.

"The man on whom you see the Spirit come down and remain is He who will baptize with the Holy Spirit. I have seen and I testify that this is the Son of God." John 1:33-34

Man baptizes you with water, and Jesus baptizes you with the Spirit.

"He will baptize you with the Holy Spirit and with fire." Luke 3:16

In the Book of I Samuel, Samuel is telling Saul that the Lord has chosen him to be king. In telling Him how the Spirit of the Lord will come upon him and change him, is how we are changed upon being baptized in the Holy Spirit.

"The Spirit of the Lord will come upon you in power, and you will prophesy with them, and you will be changed into a different person." I Samuel 10:6

The Holy Spirit of the Lord in us sanctifies us.

"God chose you to be saved through the sanctifying work of the Spirit and through belief in the truth." II Thessalonians 2:13

Being washed in the blood of Jesus, our sins are forgiven and we are now holy in the sight of God. Jesus was holy and was without sin, so in turn, when we receive Him, we are as well.

"Sanctify them by the truth; Your Word is truth. As you sent me into the world, I have sent them into the world. For them, I sanctify Myself, that they too may be truly sanctified." John 17:17-19

The Holy Spirit within us helps us to continue to be holy. The Holy Spirit will lead and guide you through all your trials, through the still small voice of the Lord within your heart.

"But when He, the Spirit of truth comes, He will guide you into all truth. He will not speak on His own; He will speak only what He hears, and He will tell you what is yet to come." John 16:13

We have to 'die' to our sinful nature, as long as we are in this world; every day. Through the trials we go through, as we depend on God and spend time with Him in prayer and through reading His Word, we grow closer to God. We learn the truths and promises that He reveals to us in His Word. That, the spiritual gifts given to us by the Lord, and the fruit of His Spirit help us to endure and persevere through our trials and to help others in their trials.

"And we rejoice in the hope of the glory of God. Not only so, but we also rejoice in our sufferings, because we know that suffering produces perseverance; perseverance, character; character, and hope. And hope does not disappoint us, because God has poured out His love into our hearts by the Holy Spirit, whom He has given us." Romans 5:2-5

Our Heavenly Father sends the Holy Spirit, and the fruit of the Spirit indwells in us, upon receiving Jesus into our hearts.

"But the fruit of the Spirit is love, joy, peace, patience, kindness, goodness, faithfulness, gentleness, and self-control." Galatians 5:22-23

This is how in Christ we are a new creation. The fruit of His Spirit within us, and going through our trials, we are changed into who God wants us to be.

"And by that will, we have been made holy through the sacrifice of the body of Jesus Christ once for all." Hebrews 10:10

In the Book of II Kings, the men of the city of Jericho told Elisha that the water was bad and the land was unproductive. This is how we all are before we receive Jesus. We are not filled with the fruit of His Spirit; therefore, we bear no fruit. Our life is not a light to the world. Elisha told them to bring him a 'new bowl' in which he put salt in it and threw it into the spring. The water was healed. In receiving Jesus, that 'new bowl' is us as a new creation in Christ. We are called to be the 'salt of the earth.'

"Everyone will be salted with fire. Salt is good, but if it loses its saltiness, how can you make it salty again? Have salt in yourselves, and be at peace with each other." Mark 9:49-50

Our lives are supposed to show people in the way we live; that we are Spirit-filled Christians, by the fruit of the Spirit of Jesus within us. It shows Jesus is the Lord of our lives. Therefore our life should be a witness to the world that Jesus does exist. The Holy Spirit gives life to your soul and we are called to witness and testify to that life. The Holy Spirit within you will change and transform you into the Lord's image as you continue to surrender to God and stay in His Word.

"And we, who with unveiled faces all reflect the Lord's glory, are being transformed into His likeness with ever-increasing glory, which comes from the Lord, who is the Spirit." II Corinthians 3:18

Loving, forgiving, humility, obedience, and patience are fruit of the Holy Spirit and these qualities will not be something you make yourself do. These qualities will become who you are and will be evident to all who know you. The life that you live as you walk in the Spirit every day will be a better witness to those around you than your words.

As the Lord told Moses, in the Book of Deuteronomy, to choose a place for Him to dwell, through Jesus He dwells within your heart. And as He traveled with the Israelites in a cloud by day and a pillar of fire at night, so will the Holy Spirit be with you. The Holy Spirit will lead you, guide you, and comfort you as well.

"Praise be to the God and Father of our Lord Jesus Christ, the Father of compassion and the God of all comfort, who comforts us in all our troubles so that we can comfort those in any trouble with the comfort we ourselves have received from God." II Corinthians 1:3-4

Learning the promises of God and how much He really loves you and through the gifts and guidance of the Holy Spirit, also helps us to be the witnesses that we are all called to be.

"Go into all the world and preach the good news to all creation. Whoever believes and is baptized will be saved, but whoever does not believe will be condemned. And these signs will accompany those who believe: In My name, they will drive out demons; they will speak in tongues; they will pick

up snakes with their hands; and when they drink deadly poison, it will not hurt them at all; they will place their hands on sick people, and they will get well." Mark 16:15-18

In the Book of Acts, it tells of how Paul was converted, he began to preach the word of God boldly! This is from someone who used to persecute Christians! Now he was trying to lead people to salvation to become Christians!

"After they prayed, the place where they were meeting was shaken. And they were all filled with the Holy Spirit and spoke the Word of God boldly." Acts 4:31

This is how the Holy Spirit also strengthens you and changes you.

"I pray that out of His glorious riches, He may strengthen you with power through His Spirit in your inner being, so that Christ may dwell in your hearts through faith." Ephesians 3:16-17

The Holy Spirit within us strengthens us and encourages us. You can feel the presence of His Spirit within you, and knowing that He is there and that He loves you and will guide you helps to increase your faith, bringing peace to your heart.

"Then the Church throughout Judea, Galilee, and Samaria enjoyed a time of peace. It was strengthened; and encouraged by the Holy Spirit; it grew in numbers, living in the fear of the Lord." Acts 9:31

3

∾

Baptism Of The Holy Spirit

When we ask Jesus into our hearts, we are indwelt with His Spirit, and at His appointed time He will baptize us with His Holy Spirit or we receive the power of the Holy Spirit.

"John baptized with water, but you will be baptized with the Holy Spirit." Acts 11:16

Just as Saul, David, and Paul were anointed by God with the power of the Holy Spirit, you can be too.

"If you then, though you are evil, know how to give good gifts to your children, how much more will your Father in heaven give the Holy Spirit to those who ask Him!" Luke 11:13

God wants everyone to be a witness for Him, and we are not to be ashamed of it.

"If anyone is ashamed of Me and My Words in this adulterous and sinful generation, the Son of Man will be ashamed of him when He comes in His Father's glory with the holy angels." Mark 8:38

In being baptized with the Holy Spirit, as I quoted earlier in Mark 16:15-18 and Luke 3:16, there will be signs that accompany the baptism.

"Tongues, then, are a sign, not for believers but for unbelievers; prophecy, however, is for believers, not for unbelievers." I Corinthians 14:22

"All of them were filled with the Holy Spirit and began to speak in other tongues as the Spirit enabled them." Acts 2:4

Many people think that these things do not happen today, that it was just for the days of Paul. That is not so. Some use this verse as a reference:

"Love never fails. But where there are prophecies, they will cease; where there are tongues, they will be stilled; where there is knowledge, it will pass away. For we know in part and we prophecy in part, but when perfection comes, the imperfect disappears." I Corinthians 13:8-10

Jesus was perfect. But Paul is speaking here after Jesus had already come! He is talking about our own perfection. For here on earth as we live in the human body, we will always 'fall short.' We will not reach perfection until we get to heaven. Neither was he speaking of the completion of the New Testament. Paul was writing as the Spirit led him to instruct the people of the different places he traveled to. He did not even know that he was writing the New Testament. We need to take all Scripture together, not just in parts.

"I want to know Christ and the power of His resurrection and the fellowship of sharing in His sufferings, becoming like Him in His death, and so, somehow, to attain the resurrection from the dead. Not that I have already obtained all this, or have already been made perfect, but I press on to take hold of that for which Christ Jesus took hold of me. Brothers, I do not consider myself yet to have taken hold of it. But one thing I do: Forgetting what is behind and straining toward what is ahead, I press on toward the

goal to win the prize for which God has called me heavenward in Christ Jesus." Philippians 3:10-14

We will not reach perfection until we get to heaven, until then we need all the spiritual gifts that the Lord wants to bless us with. We need them to help increase our knowledge and wisdom of the Bible, to help us with our Christian walk on earth, and to help us in witnessing to others, leading them to the wonderful gift of salvation! Just as the Spirit of Jesus never changes, neither does His Spirit within us or the gifts that He gives us.

"Jesus Christ is the same yesterday and today and forever." Hebrews 13:8

If Jesus is the same yesterday, today, and forever, so is His Holy Spirit and the anointing He places on everyone born into the family of God.

If you read the Book of Leviticus, it talks about Pentecost. Pentecost is celebrated 50 days after the night of Passover. The Passover was celebrated when the Israelites were in bondage to the Egyptians. Everyone who had the blood of a year-old lamb without defect smeared over the top and sides of their door frames would be safe. The angel of the Lord was to pass through the streets and every firstborn child of any family that did not have this on their doors would be put to death.

All the Israelites were warned of this and if they obeyed their lives would be spared. Just as you and I are warned of the consequences of living a life of sin. It is an eternity in hell. God loves us and warns us of this and tells us what to do to be saved. If we do not heed His warnings, it is our fault and not His.

Passover represents leaving our life of sin behind, dying to our sins, and being born again into the family of God. Just as the Lord saved them from death, He saved us from eternal damnation when He died on the cross at Calvary.

Pentecost represents the deliverance of the people from their bondage of slavery to the Egyptians. Just as every one of us who receives Jesus is delivered from the bondage of sin. We are harvested into the family of God. During the celebration of Pentecost, they were to offer a burnt offering and a drink offering. This represents the body and blood of Jesus Christ who was offered up for our sins.

They were also to offer a **first fruit** offering. This represents Jesus who was our first fruit. He was the first to rise from the dead and upon His resurrection into heaven, His Holy Spirit was made available to all who believe and receive. We receive the fruit of His Spirit. This also represents how we are to put Him. We are to put Him first, we are to greet the day and end the day talking to the Lord. Just as the Israelites were to offer up a sin offering in the morning and the evening. We are also to give Him the first fruits of our pay. Not second. He is the One who provides us with work and supplies all our needs. We are to trust Him for that.

"The Lord is my Shepherd; I shall not be in want. He makes me lie down in green pastures, He leads me beside quiet waters, He restores my soul." Psalm 23:1-2

If you are not in want, then there is nothing that you need. All your needs are met.

Many people are confused about the baptism of the Holy Spirit and wonder what happens to you at conversion.

"Therefore go and make disciples of all nations, baptizing them in the name of the Father and of the Son and of the Holy Spirit, and teaching them to obey everything I have commanded you. And surely I am with you always, to the very end of the age." Matthew 28:19-20

"May the grace of the Lord Jesus Christ, and the love of God, and the fellowship of the Holy Spirit be with you all." II Corinthians 13:14

At conversion, we are indwelt with the Spirit of Jesus.

"Because you are sons, God sent the Spirit of His Son into our hearts, the Spirit who calls out, 'Abba, Father.' So you are no longer a slave, but a son; and since you are a son, God has made you also an heir." Galatians 4:6-7

"Thus, being "born again...". "I tell you the truth, no one can see the kingdom of God unless he is born again." John 3:3

We are made alive with Christ in this.

"But because of His great love for us, God, who is rich in mercy, made us alive with Christ even when we were dead in transgressions-- it is by grace you have been saved." Ephesians 2:4-5

It is just like drinking a glass of water. The water is in you as you drink it. So it is when you become a Christian and are indwelt with the Spirit of Jesus at conversion. When you are baptized with the Holy Spirit, receiving power from above, it is like being totally immersed in water; like going swimming. When you swim under water you are totally immersed in the water.

Another way to look at it is the wiring in the wall of your house. The wiring runs through walls, but if you do not flip the switch on there will not be any light. The Holy Spirit within us at conversion is the wiring and Jesus flipping the switch on is the baptism of the Holy Spirit. Jesus turns on the power to what is already in you. That is what it is to be baptized in the Holy Spirit. We receive His Spirit at conversion, but when we are baptized it is like receiving the 2nd portion of the Spirit. Peter said it like this:

"Because the Holy Spirit had not yet come upon any of them; they had simply been baptized into the name of the Lord Jesus. Then Peter and John placed their hands on them, and they received the Holy Spirit." Acts 8:16-17

They were saying that they had asked Jesus into their hearts but the baptism as spoken of in Acts 1:8 had not happened yet. The Holy Spirit empowers us to speak in tongues, heal people, drive out demons, etc., as the Lord God decides to distribute these gifts to us.

"But you will receive power when the Holy Spirit comes on you." Acts 1:8

As we are obedient to God, submitting to His will and reading the Bible our minds are renewed day by day.

"Do not conform any longer to the pattern of this world, but be transformed by the renewing of your mind." Romans 12:2

The indwelling of the Spirit of Jesus helps us to walk in the Spirit. The fruit of His Spirit shows through.

"You, however, are controlled not by the sinful nature but by the Spirit, if the Spirit of God lives in you. And if anyone does not have the Spirit of Christ, he does not belong to Christ." Romans 8:9

There is only one baptism of the Holy Spirit.

"Make every effort to keep the unity of the Spirit through the bond of peace. There is one body and one Spirit--just as you were called to one hope when you were called--one Lord, one faith, one baptism; one God and Father of all, who is over all and through all and in all." Ephesians 4:3-6

When you are born again, God united Himself with you through the Holy Spirit and you become one, thus "one with Him in spirit."

"But he who unites himself with the Lord is one with Him in spirit." I Corinthians 6:17

You are not two beings, but one.

"For we were baptized by one Spirit into one body—whether Jews or Greeks slave or free—and we were all given the one Spirit to drink." I Corinthians 12:13

Being baptized in the Holy Spirit is simply filling you to the fullest; completing what He began:

"For in Christ all the fullness of the Deity lives in bodily form, and you have been given fullness in Christ, who is the head over every power and authority. In Him you were also circumcised, in the putting off of the sinful nature not with a circumcision done by the hands of men but with the circumcision done by Christ, having been buried with Him in baptism and raised with Him through your faith in the power of God, who raised Him from the dead." Colossians 2:9-12

This baptism, not the water baptism done by your Pastor, is done by Jesus Christ. Baptism of the Holy Spirit is given to us by Jesus Christ and when He chooses to bestow it on us. It is to turn the power of the Holy Spirit that is already in us. Another explanation is when you put fuel in a car it is in the tank, but the car will not turn on until you turn the key in the ignition switch. Again, Jesus is just flipping the switch.

"I baptize you with water for repentance. But after me will come one who is more powerful than I, whose sandals I am not fit to carry. He will baptize you with the Holy Spirit and with fire." Matthew 3:11

As we are obedient and earnestly seek the baptism upon His will, His timing, not ours, we are baptized with the Holy Spirit.

"We are witnesses of these things, and so is the Holy Spirit, whom God has given to those who obey him." Acts 5:32

As a result of being baptized in the Holy Spirit, you are filled with the Holy Spirit and the power of the Holy Spirit.

"Then Peter, filled with the Holy Spirit, said to them: 'Rulers and elders of the people! If we are being called to account today for an act of kindness shown to a cripple and are asked how he was healed, then know this, you and all the people of Israel: it is by the name of Jesus Christ of Nazareth, whom you crucified but whom God raised from the dead, that this man stands before you healed." Acts 4:8-10

In the Old Testament when the Israelites were building the Tabernacle, God did not fill the Tabernacle with His Spirit until the work was completed.

"Then Moses set up the courtyard around the tabernacle and altar and put up the curtain at the entrance to the courtyard. And so Moses finished the work. Then the cloud covered the Tent of Meeting, and the glory of the Lord filled the tabernacle." Exodus 40:33-34

Everything had to be in order. God is not a God of disorder.

"For God is not a God of disorder but of peace." Exodus 40:33-34

That is why in giving Moses the measurements in building the Tabernacle, everything had to be exact. So it is with us and our walk with God. He will not inhabit anything or anyone unclean.

"Do you not know that your body is a temple of the Holy Spirit, who is in you, whom you have received from God? You are not your own; you were bought at a price. Therefore honor God with your body." I Corinthians 6:19-20

Also as you read in the Old Testament you will see that any time anyone died or was diseased, they had to be put outside the city. They were considered "unclean." As our hearts and minds are renewed, at the appropriate time set forth by God, if you faint not and keep asking, you will be baptized with the Holy Spirit. Just keep obeying God and walking in the fruit of His Spirit and keep asking Him. You will be baptized because it is a promise for all Christians.

"You do not have, because you do not ask God." James 4:2

The Israelites were also called to offer a new grain offering at Pentecost as well, a wave offering. As the Jews offered up a new grain offering to the Lord, He in turn is our bread of life.

"I am the bread of life. He who comes to Me will never go hungry, and he who believes in Me will never be thirsty." John 6:35

He will not only meet our physical needs, but our spiritual needs as well. A wave offering signifies fellowship between you and Jesus Christ and the peace you receive once you are saved. The new grain offering consisted of 2 loaves of bread made with 2 tenths of an ephah of fine flour baked with yeast. These 2 loaves represent the Jews in which Jesus offered salvation to them first and then the Gentiles. They were made with yeast, which represents sin. Meaning we can come to Jesus as sinners and ask for forgiveness and receive His Holy Spirit into our hearts.

"But God demonstrates His own love for us in this: While we were still sinners, Christ died for us." Romans 5:8

They were made with 2 tenths of an ephah of fine flour. "Fine flour" is a representation of the perfect, sinless life of Jesus Christ. It was to be mixed with oil, which is a representation of the Holy Spirit. They were to add salt to their offering as well.

"Season all your grain offerings with salt. Do not leave the salt of the covenant of your God out of your grain offerings; add salt to all your offerings." Leviticus 2:13

Salt is a symbol of the permanence of the Holy Spirit.

"Whatever is set aside from the holy offerings the Israelites present to the Lord I give to you and your sons and daughters as your regular share. It is an everlasting covenant of salt before the Lord for both you and your offspring." Numbers 18:19

It is also a symbol of the power of the Holy Spirit and how it enlightens you and enables you to speak boldly.

"Let your conversation be always full of grace, seasoned with salt, so that you may know how to answer everyone." Colossians 4:6

"Now, Lord, consider their threats and enable your servants to speak your word with great boldness. Stretch out your hand to heal and perform miraculous signs and wonders through the name of your holy servant Jesus." Acts 4:29-30

They were also to use 2 tenths of an ephah of fine flour. Regular grain offerings were made with only 1 tenth.

"A tenth of an ephah of fine flour as a regular grain offering, half of it in the morning and half in the evening. Prepare it with oil on a griddle." Leviticus 6:20-21

These 2 tenths mean a double portion of His Holy Spirit is available to us. Just as Elisha asked Elijah for a double portion of his spirit before Elijah was taken up to heaven. The way Elijah was taken up in a chariot of fire and a whirlwind; this is the way the Holy Spirit comes on us when we are baptized in the Holy Spirit. Fire and wind symbolize the Holy Spirit.

"Suddenly a sound like the blowing of a violent wind came from heaven and filled the whole house where they were sitting. They saw what seemed to be tongues of fire that separated and came to rest on each of them. All of them were filled with the Holy Spirit and began to speak in other tongues as the Spirit enabled them." Acts 2:2-4

"Let me inherit a double portion of your spirit,' Elisha replied. 'You have asked a difficult thing,' Elijah said, 'yet if you see me when I am taken from you, it will be yours-- otherwise not.' As they were walking along and talking together, suddenly a chariot of fire and horses of fire appeared and separated the two of them, and Elijah went up to heaven in a whirlwind." II Kings 2:9-11

We can receive a double portion as well. First at receiving the indwelling of His Spirit into our hearts at conversion, then at the baptism of the Holy Spirit in which we are totally filled with His Spirit and the power of the Spirit. We just need to see with our hearts; and believe. This is what is symbolized when Elijah asks Elisha if he saw him when he was taken.

The first baptisms were given to the disciples and then to the people they started preaching to; they were "born again" as Jesus breathed on them when He appeared to them after His resurrection and before He ascended into heaven.

"Peace be with you! As the Father has sent Me, I am sending you.' And with that, He breathed on them and said, 'Receive the Holy Spirit. If you

forgive anyone his sins, they are forgiven; if you do not forgive them, they are not forgiven." John 20:21-23

The disciples had to wait until Jesus ascended into heaven.

"Do not leave Jerusalem, but wait for the gift My Father promised, which you have heard Me speak about. For John baptized with water, but in a few days you will be baptized with the Holy Spirit." Acts 1:4-5

This shows that Jesus told them to wait. It is up to Jesus when we receive it; some of the people they preached to upon believing received it at once. Jesus says to "ask and you will receive," and you will for "the Lord is faithful to all His promises and loving toward all He has made;" when is up to Him.

"When the day of Pentecost came, they were all together in one place. Suddenly a sound like the blowing of a violent wind came from heaven and filled the whole house where they were sitting. They saw what seemed to be tongues of fire that separated and came to rest on each of them." Acts 2:1-3

This is when the disciples were baptized with the Holy Spirit. The Lord will baptize us according to how He chooses, big and bold or like a bolt of love and joy hitting our hearts all at once.

"I am gentle and humble in heart, and you will find rest for your souls." Matthew 11:29

As with our own faith, some of us are stronger in faith than others. The Lord may use more vivid ways of showing someone with new or weak faith that He is there for them than with someone with strong faith.

"O Lord, you have searched me and you know me. You know when I sit and when I rise; you perceive my thoughts from afar. You discern my going

out and my lying down; you are familiar with all my ways. Before a word is on my tongue you know it completely, O Lord." Psalm 139:1-4

I believe that this is the reason why the Holy Spirit came on so many people all at once back then and in the way it did. Others did not receive it at the time of their conversion.

"There he found some disciples and asked them, 'Did you receive the Holy Spirit when you believed?' They answered, 'No, we have not even heard that there is a Holy Spirit." Acts 19:1-2

At that, Paul placed his hands on them.

"When Paul placed his hands on them, the Holy Spirit came on them, and they spoke in tongues and prophesied." Acts 19:6

The baptism of the Holy Spirit is for all who believe.

"Repent and be baptized, every one of you, in the name of Jesus Christ for the forgiveness of your sins. And you will receive the gift of the Holy Spirit. The promise is for you and your children and for all who are far off--for all whom the Lord our God will call." Acts 3:38-39

"When the apostles in Jerusalem heard that Samaria had accepted the Word of God, they sent Peter and John to them. When they arrived, they prayed for them that they might receive the Holy Spirit because the Holy Spirit had not yet come upon any of them; they had simply been baptized into the name of the Lord Jesus." Acts 8:14-16

There are reasons why some people have never received the baptism of the Holy Spirit; one is lack of faith.

"But when he asks, he must believe and not doubt, because he who doubts is like a wave of the sea, blown and tossed by the wind. That man should

not think he will receive anything from the Lord; he is a double-minded man, unstable in all he does." James 1:6-7

"And without faith, it is impossible to please God." Hebrews 11:6

You must believe in God and the promises He gives us in the Bible. We cannot take bits and pieces of the Bible to believe for our own choosing; just because we have never seen some of the things mentioned in the Bible. We have never seen God yet we believe in Him. What is the difference? That is not what faith is; faith believes without seeing.

"So do not throw away your confidence; it will be richly rewarded. You need to persevere so that when you have done the will of God, you will receive what He has promised." Hebrews 10:35-36

"Now faith is being sure of what we hope for and certain of what we do not see." Hebrews 11:1

Another reason may be that Jesus simply does not think you are ready to receive it yet.

"Anyone who lives on milk, being still an infant, is not acquainted with the teaching about righteousness. But solid food is for the mature, who by constant use have trained themselves to distinguish good from evil." Hebrews 5:13-14

"Therefore let us leave the elementary teachings about Christ and go on to maturity, not laying again the foundation of repentance from acts that lead to death, and of faith in God, instruction about baptisms, the laying on of hands, the resurrection of the dead, and eternal judgment. And God permitting, we will do so." Hebrews 6:1-3

4

Sealed!

At your conversion, the moment you asked Jesus into your heart, you were sealed by God. You became a child of God.

"Having believed, you were marked in Him with a seal, the promised Holy Spirit, who is a deposit guaranteeing our inheritance until the redemption of those who are God's possession--to the praise of His glory." Ephesians 1:13-14

That is awesome to me! Knowing that now, I belong to God. I am His child and as I will always be there to love, protect, and see to all the needs of my son, God will always be there for us. He is the one who anoints us with the Holy Spirit. That anointing and the feeling in your heart that lets you know that God is with you is very comforting. The Creator of the universe loves us all and with God as our Father, there is nothing impossible to him who believes.

"Everything is possible for him who believes." Mark 9:23

The purpose of God sealing us is that now we are certain that we are

God's own, guaranteeing our security that we are preserved as a child of God until the day of redemption.

"Now it is God who makes both us and you stand firm in Christ. He anointed us, set His seal of ownership on us, and put His Spirit in our hearts as a deposit, guaranteeing what is to come." II Corinthians 1:21-22

We may get down and discouraged from time to time due to the trials that we are going through, but praise God; because we are His He will never let us stay down! He will not let us be harmed.

"They were told not to harm the grass of the earth or any plant or tree, but only those people who did not have the seal of God on their foreheads." Revelation 9:4

In your Christian walk, you will have troubles, but rest in the fact that God loves you and will always be with you. Reading His Word will help you to know His promises and the will for your life. Put them into practice. Just like when you go to the doctor when you are sick. If He gives you medicine, it can only help you if you take it. The Lord wants to bless you and wants you to grow as a Christian. But if you do not talk with Him and read His Book of Instructions for your life, you will be making mistakes that you could have prevented with a little understanding from the Bible.

"And do not grieve the Holy Spirit of God, with whom you were sealed for the day of redemption." Ephesians 4:30

Read His Word and study it. It will only benefit you. But remember you have to read all of it, it goes together.

"Do not add to what I command you and do not subtract from it, but keep the commands of the Lord your God that I give you." Deuteronomy 4:2

You can't take parts of it to suit your own needs.

"I warn everyone who hears the words of the prophecy of this book: If anyone adds anything to them, God will add to him the plagues described in this book. And if anyone takes words away from this book of prophecy, God will take away from him his share in the tree of life and in the holy city, which is described in this book." Revelation 22:18-19

The whole Bible fits together for our good and our protection, to help us through life and we are to follow all His commands.

"See that you do all I command you; do not add to it or take away from it." Deuteronomy 12:32

All of it is true.

"Sanctify them by the truth; your Word is truth." John 17:17

It is all from God to bless us.

"All Scripture is God-breathed and is useful for teaching, rebuking, correcting and training in righteousness, so that the man of God may be thoroughly equipped for every good work." II Timothy 3:16-17

The Word of God was given to us to bless us and to help us go through life with all the love and encouragement that God can give us.

"Praise the Lord. Blessed is the man who fears the Lord, who finds great delight in His commands." Psalm 112:1

He did not leave us down here to walk blindly without help.

"For the Word of God is living and active. Sharper than any double-edge

sword, it penetrates even to dividing soul and spirit, joints and marrow; it judges the thoughts and attitudes of the heart." Hebrews 4:12

We can put out the Spirit's fire within us if we are not careful.

"Do not put out the Spirit's fire; do not treat prophecies with contempt." I Thessalonians 5:19

In staying close to God in prayer and through his Bible we are better equipped with the knowledge we need to stay away from the temptations Satan throws our way. God redeemed us to bless us and the Bible will help us to learn how to stay close to God and how to grow as a Christian.

"He redeemed us so that the blessing given to Abraham might come to the Gentiles through Christ Jesus, so that by faith we might receive the promise of the Spirit." Galatians 3:14

Our Heavenly Father loves us so much, no one really knows just how much, but we can take comfort in knowing that He does love us.

"Great is the Lord and most worthy of praise; His greatness no one can fathom." Psalm 145:3

5

∾

Annointing

Out of God's overwhelming love for us, He calls each of us into the ministry He has for us and He anoints us to perform it.

"But you have an anointing from the Holy One, and all of you know the truth." I John 2:20

We are given an anointing for the call on our life that He has for us. This anointing is the ability to do whatever task or ministry that He has for us.

"As for you, the anointing you received from Him remains in you, and you do not need anyone to teach you. But as His anointing teaches you about all things and as that anointing is real, not counterfeit--just as it has taught you, remain in Him." I John 2:27

The ability will be easy for us, but for someone else, it may be diffi-cult. Just like David when he was about to go up against Goliath. King Saul gave him his armor and it did not fit. The anointing God has for me will not be like the anointing He has for you. The calling He has for you may be to sing, preach, or evangelize in order to reach the world outside the church, or even write.

"But when they arrest you, do not worry about what to say or how to say it. At that time you will be given what to say, for it will not be you speaking, but the Spirit of your Father speaking through you." Matthew 10:19-20

As you grow in your Christian walk and stay close to God in prayer, Bible study, and obedience He will reveal His will and call for your life by the desires and inspirations He gives you in your heart.

"May He give you the desire of your heart and make all your plans succeed." Psalm 20:4

"Delight yourself in the Lord and He will give you the desires of your heart." Psalm 37:4

6

∾

Gifts Of The Holy Spirit

There are different kinds of gifts all of which are given to us by the grace of God through the Holy Spirit. Some are given to us at the time we receive the Spirit of Jesus within us. Some are not given until we are baptized with the Holy Spirit. This again depends on Jesus, His purpose for you, and if He thinks you are ready for it. How is your love walk? Is it full of the flesh and the 'what about me's'?

Love is what compelled Jesus in everything He did and is needed to use the gift of encouragement, service, teaching, hospitality, and the gift of healing. There can be no flesh, Jesus and His purpose and glory is always first. Would you want your 9-year-old child driving your car? No! He is not mature enough, old enough, or experienced enough to handle it. So it is with the gift of the Holy Spirit. If you are not mature enough in your Christian walk, meaning you still have a lot of flesh, you would be more apt to misuse certain more powerful gifts, thus not using them for God's glory.

Being baptized in the Holy Spirit is a matter of yielding and faith, not age. Nor is it about how perfect a Christian you are in your daily walk. As long as we live in the flesh there will be times that we mess up. You will be baptized it is a promise and a gift and will come when you persevere in asking, believe God, and do not let fear rule over you.

"Consider it pure joy, my brothers, whenever you face trials of many kinds because you know that the testing of your faith develops perseverance. Perseverance must finish its work so that you may be mature and complete, not lacking anything." James 1:2-4

To be mature in your faith you have been purified, or have undergone the baptism of fire.

"I baptize you with water for repentance. But after me will come one who is more powerful than I, whose sandals I am not fit to carry. He will baptize you with the Holy Spirit and with fire." Matthew 3:11

God likens the process of purification to the purifying process of gold. When gold is purified it goes through the fire until the goldsmith can see his image in it.

"Praise be to the God and Father of our Lord Jesus Christ! In his great mercy, he has given us new birth into a living hope through the resurrection of Jesus Christ from the dead, and into an inheritance that can never perish, spoil, or fade—kept in heaven for you, who through faith are shielded by God's power until the coming of the salvation that is ready to be revealed in the last time. In this, you greatly rejoice, though now for a little while you may have had to suffer grief in all kinds of trials. These have come so that your faith—of greater worth than gold, which perishes even though refined by fire—may be proved genuine and may result in praise, glory, and honor when Jesus Christ is revealed." I Peter 1:3-7

God wants to see His image in you! We should be a reflection of our Lord and Savior! This gives true glory to God; the world is affected more by your life than your words.

"And we, who with unveiled faces all reflect the Lord's glory, are being

transformed into His likeness with ever-increasing glory, which comes from the Lord, who is the Spirit." II Corinthians 3:18

In the Book of Daniel 3:20-27, Shadrach, Meshach, and Abednego are thrown into a fiery furnace and they came forth unharmed! In fact, people saw a 4th man in the fire with them, a man that looks like "a son of the gods." This was Jesus! This passage represents the purification process of God. The Lord has years of the world to "weed" out of most of us when we are saved.

"He replied, Every plant that my heavenly Father has not planted will be pulled up by the roots." Matthew 15:13

Yes, we are a new creation, but our minds need to be renewed.

"Do not conform any longer to the pattern of this world, but be transformed by the renewing of your mind. Then you will be able to test and approve what God's will is—His good, pleasing, and perfect will." Romans 12:2

In submitting to the "baptism of fire" God will purify your heart removing the impurities and you will "come forth as gold," and ready to move on to the next stage in your walk giving all glory to God as He deserves. If want to be greatly used by God as He promises, "You will do even greater things than these" then you will have to go through the fire; if you want to share in the glory, in the inheritance then you have to share in the sufferings; the trials.

"Now if we are children, then we are heirs—heirs of God and co-heirs with Christ, if indeed we share in His sufferings in order that we may also share in His glory." Romans 8:17

In letting God purify you—you are also learning how to be led by the Spirit.

"Those who belong to Christ Jesus have crucified the sinful nature with its passions and desires. Since we live by the Spirit, let us keep in step with the Spirit." Galatians 5:24-25

This is day-to-day dying to self.

"If anyone would come after Me, he must deny himself and take up his cross daily and follow Me." Luke 9:23

"For to me, to live is Christ and to die is gain." Philippians 1:21

If you ever want to be used mightily in your daily life for God, you need to remember it is for His glory and not your own and you must let the Holy Spirit lead you; not your mind, will, and emotions. This is submitting to the Lordship of Christ. Your flesh and your mind may want to do something contrary to the Spirit, but it is your choice to obey it or God.

"The spiritual man makes judgments about all things, but he himself is not subject to any man's judgment: 'For who has known the mind of the Lord that he may instruct Him?' But we have the mind of Christ." I Corinthians 2:15

You are doing God's will and it is for His purpose and glory and He already knows the outcome; therefore He already knows the process and steps He wants to take to achieve it. The purification process is also known as sanctification.

"May God Himself, the God of peace, sanctify you through and through. May your whole spirit, soul, and body be kept blameless at the coming of our Lord Jesus Christ." I Thessalonians 5:23

Ignorance of the baptism, fear, and your daily Christian walk is lacking love are three of the biggest hindrances to receiving the baptism of the Holy Spirit and I believe that fear and unbelief go hand in hand. Love is the driving force behind everything God has done for us and without love, the Holy Spirit will not manifest Himself through you. Having no love blocks the flow of His love working through you. If you are fearful then you are not trusting in God.

"And without faith, it is impossible to please God, because anyone who comes to Him must believe that He exists and that He rewards those who earnestly seek Him." Hebrews 11:6

Some people may be baptized the moment they are saved while others may be saved for 5 or 10 years before receiving it! Baptism of the Holy Spirit can come to a young child or an adult. John the Baptist was baptized at birth.

"Then an angel of the Lord appeared to him, standing at the right side of the altar of incense. When Zechariah saw him, he was startled and was gripped with fear. But the angel said to him, 'Do not be afraid, Zechariah; your prayer has been heard. Your wife Elizabeth will bear you a son, and you are to give him the name John. He will be a joy and delight to you, and many will rejoice because of his birth, for he will be great in the sight of the Lord. He is never to take wine or other fermented drink, and he will be filled with the Holy Spirit even from birth." Luke 1:11-15

Acts 2:17 tells of how the Lord will pour out His Spirit on our sons and daughters and in Matthew 18:3 tells of how we must have the faith of a child because children trust their parents completely. Samuel was just a boy when, while at Eli's house learning under his authority, that he first heard the voice of the Lord. David was just a young boy when he was anointed to be king and still a young boy when through the help of the Lord defeated Goliath, a man of 9 feet tall! Age does not matter! It is the willingness to yield and surrender completely to the Holy Spirit and let Him move or speak through you that makes the difference.

"I am the Lord; that is My name! I will not give My glory to another or My praise to idols." Isaiah 42:8

"We have different gifts, according to the grace given us." Romans 12:6

No matter what gifts that we are blessed with, God works in all of them.

"There are different kinds of working, but the same God works all of them in all men." I Corinthians 12:6

The gifts given to you upon being baptized by the Holy Spirit are for the good of all people, whether it is believers or unbelievers.

"Now to each one, the manifestation of the Spirit is given for the common good." I Corinthians 12:7

We are to love one another, and not only in words but in our actions as well. Sometimes the love that you show someone is the only way that they will see Jesus.

"Do to others as you would have them do to you. If you love those who love you, what credit is that to you?" Luke 6:31-32

"And now these three remain: faith, hope, and love. But the greatest of these is love." I Corinthians 13:13

Not everyone will have the same gift, continue on in the next two chapters to find more information on the gifts.

7

∽

Gifts Of The Holy Spirit In Depth

"I will pour out My Spirit on all people. Your sons and daughters will prophesy, your old men will dream dreams, your young men will see visions. Even on My servants, both men and women, I will pour out My Spirit in those days." Joel 2:28-29

The gifts of the Spirit are broken down into three Basic Groups which are Domata Gifts (equipping the Church or ministries), Charismata Gifts (stewardship gifts or ability gifts), and Pneumatic Charismata Gifts (spiritual gifts for dynamic manifestations of the Holy Spirit in which He openly displays Himself). There are three categories within the Pneumatic Charismata Gifts found in I Corinthians 12, which are the major gifts and they are Revelation Gifts, Vocal Gifts, and Power Gifts.

You need complete faith to operate in these gifts. The Revelation Gifts are word of wisdom, word of knowledge, and discerning of spirits. The Vocal Gifts are; speaking in tongues, interpretation of tongues, and gifts of prophecy (dreams and visions fall into this category and are found in Acts 2:17-18). If someone speaks in tongues in Church an interpreter must be present. It is to edify or build up the church.

"I would like every one of you to speak in tongues, but I would rather

have you prophesy. He who prophesies is greater than the one who speaks in tongues, unless he interprets, so that the church may be edified." I Corinthians 14:5

If one speaks in tongues in private, to himself as in praying to or praising God, he edifies himself.

"He who speaks in a tongue edifies himself, but he who prophesies edifies the church." I Corinthians 14:4

This only gives you a greater awareness that you are filled with the Holy Spirit, which increases your faith, in knowing that God is with you and loves you. The Power Gifts are faith, healing, and miracles. It does not matter what gift you have each one is needed and important. In Christ, we are all the 'body of Christ' and each part is needed to make it all complete.

"The body is a unit, though it is made up of many parts; and though all its parts are many, they form one body. So it is with Christ. For we were all baptized by one Spirit into one body--whether Jews or Greeks, slave or free-- and we were all given the one Spirit to drink." I Corinthians 12:12-13

God has given us the spiritual gifts that best fit us and we are all to work together for the good of all people and for the unity of the whole body of Christ.

"But God has combined the members of the body and has given greater honor to the parts that lacked it, so that there should be no division in the body, but that its parts should have equal concern for each other. If one part suffers, every part suffers with it; if one part is honored, every part rejoices with it." I Corinthians 12:24-26

In using any of our gifts it is not for our own good, it is to bring glory to God, to witness to unbelievers, and to strengthen the church. As the church is strengthened, it is able to do more of a service to all people in the way God intended it to be.

"What then shall we say, brothers? When you come together, everyone has a hymn, or a word of instruction, a revelation, a tongue, or an interpretation. All of these must be done for the strengthening of the church." I Corinthians 14:26

The different spiritual gifts or callings given by the Lord are found in the Book of Acts, Romans and I Corinthians and Ephesians. In the Book of Romans 12 and I Corinthians 12, list the Charismata Gifts or stewardship gifts such as teaching, serving, giving (being generous), encouragement, and leadership, and how we are all to be hospitable. It also lists the gifts of administration, the gift of helping others. The Domata Gifts or Gifts of Office are listed in the Book of Ephesians 4:11-12 are evangelists, teachers, prophets, pastors, and apostles.

8

Pneumatic Charismata Gifts Of The Holy Spirit

Revelation Gifts

Word of Wisdom- A form of spiritual guidance or the ability to apply Scripture in a situation. This is made known to you by the Holy Spirit and not natural learning.

Word of Knowledge- The ability to perceive by the Spirit what is going on in a situation or in someone's life, it is a deep knowing about something beyond explanation that can only come from God. Jesus gave a Word of Knowledge to the woman at the well as He told her in

"You are right when you say you have no husband. The fact is, you have had five husbands, and the man you now have is not your husband."
John 4:17-18

Discerning of spirits-the ability by the Spirit to detect the Spirit of God or the spirit of evil. (Ex. Acts 16 when Paul knew there was an evil spirit in the girl). In praying for others it is very beneficial in knowing the root behind the problem. You want whoever you are praying for to have divine health, healed completely, and not just the symptoms.

Example: someone wants prayer for an addiction, but if the root cause is not addressed then the addiction may arise again. Most addictions come from a lack of self-esteem, or the need to be loved. At some point in their life, they felt rejected and unloved, and the feeling that you have from being loved and knowing it is absent. They seek that feeling elsewhere. Having this gift to discern spirits can help in knowing what is behind the spirit of addiction, the spirit of pride, and so on. It can also help you in determining the true motive behind a person's actions.

Vocal Gifts

Tongues- There are 3 kinds of tongues to speak in a tongue by yourself it edifies you; giving you encouragement that you are filled to the uttermost with the Holy Spirit.

Gift of Tongues spoken in Church or fellowship meeting needing interpretation. It is God communicating with us---Acts 2:8-12- Spoken in languages understood by men-

"Then how is it that each of us hears them in his own native language? Parthians, Medes, and Elamites; residents of Mesopotamia, Judea and Cappadocia, Pontus and Asia, Phrygia and Pamphylia, Egypt and the parts of Libya near Cyrene; visitors from Rome (both Jews and converts to Judaism); Cretans and Arabs-we hear them declaring the wonders of God in our own tongues!" Amazed and perplexed, they asked one another, "What does this mean?"

I Corinthians 14:27-28—Spoken in Church for edification of the Church and it must be interpreted- this is in relation to #1. It edifies all who hear it knowing that it is a direct Word from God.

"If anyone speaks in a tongue, two—or at the most three—should speak, one at a time and someone must interpret. If there is no interpreter, the speaker should keep quiet in the church and speak to himself and God."

I Corinthians 14:2- Prayer language --No man understands & is given upon baptism of the Holy Spirit-(this is different from the gift of Tongues listed in #1)-

"For anyone who speaks in a tongue does not speak to men but to God. Indeed, no one understands him; he utters mysteries with his spirit."

Interpretation of tongues—I Corinthians 12:6 & 11-- Holy Spirit enables you to interpret a tongue spoken—

(vs. 6) *"There are different kinds of workings, but the same God works all of them in all men."*

(vs.11) *"All these are the work of one and the same Spirit, and He gives them to each one, just as He determines."*

Gift of Prophecy—(4 Realms) — They are for exhortation, edification, and comfort.

"But everyone who prophesies speaks to men for their strengthening, encouragement, and comfort." (I Corinthians 14:3)

Power Gifts

Faith Measure of Faith--Romans 12:3 & 6 – Romans 10:17—Comes by the Word

"Consequently faith comes from hearing the message, and the message is heard through the Word of Christ." (Romans 10:17)

"For by the grace given me, I say to every one of you: Do not think of yourself more highly than you ought but rather think of yourself with sober judgment, in accordance with the measure of faith God has given you......We have different gifts, according to the grace given us. If a man's gift is prophesying, let him use it in proportion to his faith." (Romans 12:3 & 6)

Fruit of Faith

"I am the true vine, and My Father is the vinedresser. Every branch in Me that does not bear fruit He takes away; and every branch that bears fruit He prunes, that it may bear more fruit. You are already clean because of the word which I have spoken to you. Abide in Me, and I in you. As the branch cannot bear fruit of itself unless it abides in the vine, neither can you, unless you abide in Me. "I am the vine, you are the branches. He who abides in Me, and I in him, bears much fruit; for without Me, you can do nothing. If anyone does not abide in Me, he is cast out as a branch and is withered; and they gather them and throw them into the fire, and they are burned. If you abide in Me, and My words abide in you, you will ask what you desire, and it shall be done for you. By this My Father is glorified, that you bear much fruit; so you will be My disciples. "As the Father loved Me,

I also have loved you; abide in My love. If you keep My commandments, you will abide in My love, just as I have kept My Father's commandments and abide in His love. "These things I have spoken to you, that My joy may remain in you, and that your joy may be full. This is My commandment, that you love one another as I have loved you. Greater love has no one than this than to lay down one's life for his friends. You are My friends if you do whatever I command you. No longer do I call you servants, for a servant does not know what his master is doing; but I have called you friends, for all things that I heard from My Father I have made known to you. You did not choose Me, but I chose you and appointed you that you should go and bear fruit and that your fruit should remain, that whatever you ask the Father in My name He may give you. These things I command you, that you love one another." (John 15:1-17)

"Let us fix our eyes on Jesus, the author, and perfecter of our faith, who for the joy set before Him endured the cross, scorning its shame, and sat down at the right hand of the throne of God." (Hebrews 12:2)

Gift of Faith- I Corinthians 12:9 -- Gift given by the Holy Spirit and is faith to believe for something with ease that would be hard for others.

"To another faith by the same Spirit, to another gift of healing by that one Spirit."

All the gifts need faith to operate in; you need to trust that whatever gifts the Lord has given you that they are from Him and whatever task in that gift He gives you to do; He will also back up. The next two gifts need the Gift of Faith to operate in them as well. You cannot force the gifts of the Spirit; you must let the Holy Spirit lead you.

Healing—I Corinthians 12:9---- "to another faith by the same Spirit, to another gift of healing by that one Spirit."

Miraculous Powers—I Corinthians 12:10—"To another miraculous powers, to another prophecy, to another distinguishing between spirits, to another speaking in different kinds of tongues and to still another the interpretation of tongues."

Gift of Prophecy- 4 Realms of the Prophetic

Prophecy- in Hebrew, it means to flow, boil, or bubble up. The Prophetic is very important to God. To prophesy is to be inspired to preach and interpret the divine will or purpose of God. Prophecy tells of something or event in the future, it also gives correction or is instructive. It may come through an individual, a sermon, or a divine revelation from any person or thing God chooses to use to reveal it to you and will always be confirmed. It may be something that you already feel in your spirit. There are false prophets out there and some unintentionally really feel they have a word from God. Before you take any prophecy to heart get confirmation from God. He may confirm it through His Word, a vision or dream, or another individual. Getting confirmation and explanation is what is meant by needing human interpretation.

(I Corinthians 14:3-5) "But everyone who prophesies speaks to men for their strengthening, encouragement, and comfort. He who speaks in a tongue edifies himself, but he who prophesies edifies the church. I would like every one of you to speak in tongues, but I would rather have you prophesy. He who prophesies is greater than one who speaks in tongues, unless he interprets, so that the church may be edified."

(I Corinthians 14:39-40) "Therefore, my brothers, be eager to prophesy and do not forbid speaking in tongue. But everything should be done in a fitting and orderly way."

They are:

1. Prophecy of Scripture-**do not need human interpretation**
2. Spirit of Prophecy----**ALL THESE**
3. Gift of prophecy----- **THREE**
4. Office of a Prophet-----**DO!**

Dreams and Visions fall into this category.

Prophecy of Scripture- Direct revelation from God- Logos Word of God and the only one in which we do not need to judge. It is the highest and purest form of communication in which man had nothing to do with; this is a biblical revelation inspired by the Holy Spirit with no human mixture; it is truth and has no error. The other 3 realms have human input and need to be judged.

(II Peter 1:20-21) "Above all, you must understand that no prophecy of Scripture came about by the prophet's own interpretation. For prophecy never had its origin in the will of man, but men spoke from God as they were carried along by the Holy Spirit."

(John 1:1-2 & 14) "In the beginning was the Word, and the Word was with God, and the Word was God. He was with God in the beginning." (vs. 14) "The Word became flesh and made His dwelling among us. We have seen His glory, the glory of the One and Only who came from the Father, full of grace and truth."

(II Timothy 3:16-17) "All Scripture is God-breathed and is useful for teaching, rebuking, correcting and training in righteousness, so that the man of God may be thoroughly equipped for every good work."

Spirit of Prophecy--This is the anointing of the Holy Spirit that enables men and women who do not have the gift of prophecy or the office of the prophet to come under the influence of the prophetic and can predict the future. Such as in dreams or visions or a knowing in your spirit. When the power of God hit in I Samuel 19, it invaded the house- everyone was prophesying, and everyone was affected! The Spirit of Prophecy can come on thousands at a time. The gift of prophecy comes on individuals instantly- a select few.

(Revelation 19:10) "At this I fell at his feet to worship him. But he said to me, "Don't do that! I am a fellow servant with you and with your brothers and sisters who hold to the testimony of Jesus. Worship God! For it is the Spirit of prophecy who bears testimony to Jesus."

(I Samuel 19:18-24) "When David had fled and made his escape, he went to Samuel at Ramah and told him all that Saul had done to him. Then he and Samuel went to Naioth and stayed there. Word came to Saul: "David is in Naioth at Ramah;" so he sent men to capture him. But when they saw a group of prophets prophesying, with Samuel standing there as their leader, the Spirit of God came upon Saul's men and they also prophesied. Saul was told about it, and he sent more men, and they prophesied too. Saul sent men a third time, and they also prophesied. Finally, he himself left for Ramah and went to the great cistern at Secu. And he asked, "Where are Samuel and David?" Over in Naioth at Ramah," they said. So Saul went to Naioth at Ramah. But the Spirit of God came even upon him, and he walked along prophesying until he came to Naioth. He stripped off his robes and also prophesied in Samuel's presence. He lay that way all that day and night. This is why people say, "Is Saul also among the prophets?"

Gift of Prophecy- Has limitation—It is to exhort, edify & comfort the body of Christ and cannot predict the future.

(I Corinthians 12:4-10) "There are different kinds of gifts, but the same Spirit. There are different kinds of service, but the same Lord. There are different kinds of working, but the same God works all of them in all men. Now to each one, the manifestation of the Spirit is given for the common good. To one there is given through the Spirit the message of wisdom, to another the message of knowledge by means of the same Spirit, to another faith by the same Spirit, to another gifts of healing by that one Spirit, to another miraculous powers, to another prophecy, to another distinguishing between spirits, to another speaking in different kinds of tongues, and to still another the interpretation of tongues."

Office of a Prophet— It is to prepare God's people for service to build up the body of Christ and are vessels chosen by God to function accurately in the Realm of:

1. Knowledge
2. Wisdom
3. Discerning of Spirits
4. Confirmation
5. Revelation
6. Predictions
7. Visions
8. Dreams

(Ephesians 2:19-20) "Consequently, you are no longer foreigners and aliens, but fellow citizens with God's people and members of God's household, built on the foundation of the apostles and prophets, with Christ Jesus himself as the chief cornerstone."

(Ephesians 4:11-16) "It was He who gave some to be apostles, some to be prophets, some to be evangelists, and some to be pastors and teachers, to prepare God's people for works of service, so that the body of Christ may

be built up until we all reach unity in the faith and in the knowledge of the Son of God and become mature, attaining to the whole measure of the fullness of Christ. Then we will no longer be infants, tossed back and forth by the waves, and blown here and there by every wind of teaching and by the cunning and craftiness of men in their deceitful scheming. Instead, speaking the truth in love, we will in all things grow up into him who is the Head, that is, Christ. From Him, the whole body joined and held together by every supporting ligament, grows and builds itself up in love, as each part does its work."

The office of a Prophet can operate in all 9 Gifts in a service and can discern spirits and who they are and can see visions and confirm ministries. Not all who prophesy are prophets.

(Acts 21:10-12) is an example of a prophet. – "After we had been there a number of days, a prophet named Agabus came down from Judea. Coming over to us, he took Paul's belt, tied his own hands and feet with it, and said, "The Holy Spirit says, 'In this way, the Jews of Jerusalem will bind the owner of this belt and will hand him over to the Gentiles.' "When we heard this, we and the people there pleaded with Paul not to go up to Jerusalem."

(Acts 13:1-5) is an example of confirmed ministry.—"In the church at Antioch there were prophets and teachers: Barnabas, Simeon called Niger, Lucius of Cyrene, Manaen (who had been brought up with Herod the tetrarch), and Saul. While they were worshiping the Lord and fasting, the Holy Spirit said, "Set apart for me Barnabas and Saul for the work to which I have called them." So after they had fasted and prayed, they placed their hands on them and sent them off. The two of them, sent on their way by the Holy Spirit, went down to Seleucia and sailed from there to Cyprus. When they arrived at Salamis, they proclaimed the word of God in the Jewish synagogues. John was with them as their helper."

All prophecy must be judged except the Prophecy of Scripture. Prophecy is a vital part of the Church.

(I Corinthians 12:3) *"Therefore I tell you that no one who is speaking by the Spirit of God says, "Jesus be cursed," and no one can say, "Jesus is Lord," except by the Holy Spirit."*

(I Corinthians 14:28-31) *"If there is no interpreter; the speaker should keep quiet in the church and speak to himself and God. Two or three prophets should speak, and the others should weigh carefully what is said. And if a revelation comes to someone who is sitting down, the first speaker should stop. For you can all prophesy in turn so that everyone may be instructed and encouraged."*

(Acts 2:16-19) *"No, this is what was spoken by the prophet Joel: "In the last days, God says, I will pour out My Spirit on all people. Your sons and daughters will prophesy, your young men will see visions, your old men will dream dreams. Even on my servants, both men and women, I will pour out My Spirit in those days, and they will prophesy. I will show wonders in the heaven above and signs on the earth below, blood and fire and billows of smoke."*

(Acts 19:6) *"When Paul placed his hands on them, the Holy Spirit came on them, and they spoke in tongues and prophesied."*

Married Ladies—Prophecy cannot operate in you **unless** you are under authority. Your husband is your authority. When under authority the gift of prophecy will be released out of you with power. If you are not married or no Father— God is your authority. If you have a father who is a Christian- He is your authority.

(I Corinthians 11:3-16) *"Now I want you to realize that the head of every man is Christ, and the head of the woman is man, and the head of Christ is God. Every man who prays or prophesies with his head covered dishonors his head. And every woman who prays or prophesies with her head uncovered dishonors her head—it is just as though her head were shaved. If*

a woman does not cover her head, she should have her hair cut off; and if it is a disgrace for a woman to have her hair cut or shaved off, she should cover her head.   A man ought not to cover his head, since he is the image and glory of God; but the woman is the glory of man. For man did not come from woman, but woman from man; neither was man created for woman, but woman for man. For this reason, and because of the angels, the woman ought to have a sign of authority on her head. In the Lord, however, woman is not independent of man, nor is man independent of woman.   For as woman came from man, so also man is born of woman. But everything comes from God. Judge for yourselves: Is it proper for a woman to pray to God with her head uncovered? Does not the very nature of things teach you that if a man has long hair, it is a disgrace to him, but that if a woman has long hair, it is her glory? For long hair is given to her as a covering. If anyone wants to be contentious about this, we have no other practice—nor do the churches of God."

(1 Corinthians 11:4-7) "Or every man who prays or prophesies with long hair dishonors his head. And every woman who prays or prophesies with no covering (of hair) on her head dishonors her head— she is just like one of the "shorn women." If a woman has no covering, let her be for now with short hair, but since it is a disgrace for a woman to have her hair shorn or shaved, she should grow it again. A man ought not to have long hair."

Prophecy in Power

1. It is vital.
2. Must be under authority.
3. Release your faith by building your measure of faith. This must be continual through dynamic prayer and word life- this will position you to prophesy.
4. Learn to operate in the anointing- it must be drawn out. **(Deuteronomy 32:13)**-in the rock! — "He made him ride on the heights

of the land and fed him with the fruit of the fields. He nourished him with honey from the rock and with oil from the flinty crag." Jesus by praise and worship and as you do it, act in faith--it will come out. He inhabits our praise. **(Psalm 22:3)** "But thou art holy, O thou that inhabits the praises of Israel."

5. Very key—you will feel the fire of God in your being and you will feel like you will explode if you do not lay hands on someone. A word like fire in you. **(Jeremiah 20:9)** "But if I say, "I will not mention Him or speak anymore in His name," His word is in my heart like a fire, a fire shut up in my I am weary of holding it in; indeed, I cannot." You will feel a joy that you cannot explain. -- **(Luke 1:14)** "He will be a joy and delight to you, and many will rejoice because of his birth."

6. Before you prophesy—Wait until the worship becomes intense-you wait for the moment when you have to!!! Learn to read the moment!!

7. Learn to discern the thoughts of the Holy Spirit— don't give up—feelings will cause you to make mistakes. Don't give up on your

8. Stir up the gift! Use it and pray in the Holy Spirit!! **(II Timothy 1:6)** "Wherefore I put thee in remembrance that thou stir up the gift of God, which is in thee by the putting on of my hands."

9. Gifts of the Spirit when in full operation, people begin to prophesy.

Dreams and Visions

1. **Dreams**—Reveal God's Plan- The plan of a Father of One who is our Creator and One who blesses us and One who disciplines in love. They may come in parables. **(Psalm 78:2)** "I will open my mouth in parables; I will utter hidden things, things from of old."

2. **Visions**—Visions reveal God's Nature- Who He is. -- Our Creator, Savior, His nature as a Father for our eternal benefit as in the visions in the book of Amos they were visions of blessings and of discipline. **(Numbers 12:6-8)** "Listen to my words: "When a prophet of the Lord is among you, I reveal Myself to him in visions, I speak to him in dreams. But this is not true of My servant Moses; he is faithful in all My house. With him I speak face to face, clearly and not in riddles; he sees the form of the Lord. Why then were you not afraid to speak against My servant Moses?"

3. **Dreams need interpreting. Visions do not.**—God reveals Himself in visions- things revealed do not need interpreting; whereas parables that symbolize something else do need to be interpreted.

The Work of the Holy Spirit and Steps to Baptism

Repent and be saved- ask Jesus into your heart. Relax; worry, fear, doubt and anxiety are not from God. It will hinder it. You must trust Him.

(Hebrews 11:6) "And without faith it is impossible to please God because anyone who comes to Him must believe that He exists and that He rewards those who earnestly seek Him."

(James 1:6-8) "But when he asks, he must believe and not doubt, because he who doubts is like a wave of the sea, blown and tossed by the wind. That man should not think he will receive anything from the Lord; he is a double-minded man, unstable in all he does."

1. Release—get rid of all preconceived ideas- Let Jesus baptize you in the Holy Spirit in His way and in His time! He wants to, He promised to, He does not lie and He is God!! Believe the promise and wait; it will come!! **(Psalm 27:14)** "Wait for the Lord; be strong and take heart and wait for the Lord." **(Psalm 145:13)** "Your kingdom is an everlasting kingdom, and your dominion endures through all generations. The Lord is faithful to all His promises and loving toward all He has made."

2. Receive—when someone gives you a gift- you really cannot claim it until you receive it, take hold of it, and open it!!

Work of the Holy Spirit

1. The Holy Spirit brings you into God's presence.

(Ephesians 2:18)

1. The Holy Spirit fills you. (Ephesians 5:18)
2. The Holy Spirit dwells in you. (Romans 8:9)
3. The Holy Spirit helps you to pray. (Romans 8:26)
4. The Holy Spirit helps you to worship God. (John 4:24) (Philippians 3:3)
5. The Holy Spirit gives you power. (Acts 1:8) (Luke 24:49)
6. The Holy Spirit gives direction to your life. (Romans 8:14)
7. The Holy Spirit appoints you to ministry. (Acts 13:2)
8. The Holy Spirit equips you for service. (Daniel 11:32)
9. The Holy Spirit convicts the world of sin. (John 16:8)
10. The Holy Spirit leads you into (John 16:13/ 14:16-17)
11. The Holy Spirit teaches you. (John 14:26)
12. The Holy Spirit places you in the body of Christ. (Ephesians 1:13)
13. The Holy Spirit glorifies Christ. (John 16:13)

14. The Holy Spirit will testify about Jesus Christ. (John 15:26)
15. The Holy Spirit reveals Jesus Christ. (John 14:21)
16. The Holy Spirit Comforts. (John 14:26)
17. The Holy Spirit Strengthens (Acts 9:31) (Psalm 29:11) (Philippians 4:13)
18. The Holy Spirit intercedes. (Romans 8:27)

The Gifts of the Holy Spirit Listed

Found in (I Corinthians 12)

Pneumatic Charismata Gifts-Major manifestation of the Spirit:

1. Tongues
2. Interpretation of Tongues
3. Gift of Prophecy (dreams & visions included)
4. Word of Wisdom
5. Word of Knowledge
6. Discerning of Spirits
7. Faith
8. Healing
9. Miraculous Powers

Pneumatic means to fill with air or wind Charismata (Charismatic) means divine inspiration. So, put together Pneumatic Charismata means to be divinely filled with the gifts given to you by the Holy Spirit.

Charismata Gifts-for Stewardship:

Found in (Romans 12:3-9)

1. Giving
2. Serving
3. Hospitality
4. Administration
5. Encouragement
6. Leadership
7. Gift of helping others
8. Gift of showing mercy

Domata Gifts- Gifts of Office:

Domata, according to Bibleworks, is translated as "dwellings," so in relation to the spiritual gifts it is gifts of dwelling or place or office.

Found in **(Ephesians 4:11-13)** and is also known as the Fivefold Ministry. To have a complete ministry in church these five offices should be present. Pastors and teachers should be a resident of the local church, but an Apostle may be the one who started the church as Paul did. He started many churches but did not reside in them. Apostles establish and bring encouragement, correction, and teaching. Evangelist is another office that adds to the local church reminding everyone of the needs of the world; and outreach to a lost world in need of a Savior. Prophets bring correction, encouragement, and divine revelation and inspiration as the Holy Spirit reveals. Teachers are needed to help you learn about and learn how to read the Bible for yourselves. They are especially needed to help new converts learn their way as they grow and mature in Christ.

1. Pastor
2. Evangelist
3. Apostle
4. Prophet
5. Teacher

Final Thoughts

It is my desire to help people to understand the love of God and to study the Word of God for themselves.

Pray as you study the Word for wisdom to understand; God will give you that in abundance! God says that if any of us lacks wisdom, we should ask and He will give it.

"If any of you lacks wisdom, let him ask of God, who gives to all liberally and without reproach, and it will be given to him." (James 1:5)

We need the Holy Spirit to make it through life; there are too many people who choose to act selfishly and with evil intent by the free will God gave them.

In our purpose and the destiny God has for us, we cannot operate without Him. After all, it is for God's glory, not ours that we have our purpose.

"For in Him we live and move and have our being, as also some of your own poets have said, 'For we are also His offspring." (Acts 17:28)

Everything we do as a child of God makes a difference and the Holy Spirit can help you do it with ease.

As you read this book, study the Word of God along with it and allow God to teach you and give you the wisdom and inspiration you need for the purpose He has for you.

If you do not know Jesus as your personal Lord and Savior, please take a few moments and read on through the next few pages.

Special Invitation

I cannot close this book without giving you the awesome privilege of becoming a child of God, a chance to have every wrong made right and every sin washed away. If you have never asked Jesus into your heart, or maybe you did but you were never sincere, please pray the prayer on the pages following. It will be the best thing you have ever done.

After you do this, find a good Church to go to if you do not have one already. Fellowshipping with other Christians will help you on your new walk in Christ. It is also a place to worship God and learn more about Him.

Tell someone! You must confess! This should be the happiest day of your life because you now know that your eternal home is in heaven! I think that is the best life insurance anyone can have, and it is free!

(Romans 10:9-10) "That if you confess with your mouth, 'Jesus is Lord,' and believe in your heart that God raised Him from the dead, you will be saved. For it is with your heart that you believe and are justified, and it is with your mouth that you confess and are saved."

Congratulations and welcome to the family of God!

God Loves You!

(Jeremiah. 31:3) "I have loved you with an everlasting love; I have drawn you with loving-kindness."

I Timothy 2:3-4 "God our Savior, who wants all men to be saved and to come to the knowledge of the truth."

He will not knock on the door of your heart forever. Will you let Him in?

Revelation 3:20 "Here I am! I stand at the door and knock. If anyone hears My voice and opens the door, I will come in and eat with him, and he with Me."

Jesus is the only way to God.
John 14:6 "I am the way, the truth, and the life. No one comes to the Father except through Me."

John 3:3 "I tell you the truth, no one can see the kingdom of God unless he is born again."

And you must make Him Lord of your life.
Matthew 6:24 "No one can serve two masters."
Matthew 7:21 "Not everyone who says to Me, 'Lord, Lord', will enter the kingdom of heaven, but only he who does the will of My Father who is in heaven."

We must leave our old ways behind.
Mark 3:25 "If a house is divided against itself, that house cannot stand."

You can't live according to the flesh and desires of the sinful nature and expect to have Jesus in your heart. He is holy. He is love. Love and Hate cannot exist together.

Ephesians 4:22-24 "You were taught, with regard to your former way of life, to put off your old self, which is being corrupted by its deceitful desires; to be made new in the attitude of your minds; and to put on the new self, created to be like God in true righteousness and holiness."

God gives you the ability to do His will. He knows it is hard.
Philippians 4:13 "I can do everything through Him who gives me strength."

Romans 3:23 "For all have sinned and fall short of the glory of God."

I John 1:9 "If we confess our sins, He is faithful and just and will forgive us our sins and purify us from all unrighteousness."

John 1:12 "Yet to all who received Him, to those who believed in His name, He gave the right to become children of God."

Romans 10:10 "For it is with your heart that you believe and are justified, and it is with your mouth that you confess and are saved."

Then after you confess and ask forgiveness and receive Jesus into your heart, you must testify (tell someone) and be baptized. In this, God is glorified, and others might be saved by your example.

II Timothy 1:8 "So do not be ashamed to testify about our Lord"

I Peter 3:21 "And this water symbolizes baptism that now saves you also-not the removal of dirt from the body but the pledge of a good conscience toward God. It saves you by the resurrection of Jesus Christ."

Invitation To Salvation Prayer

Dear Almighty Father in heaven, I know that I am a sinner and I ask your forgiveness of all my sins. I want to make You the Lord of my life and I want to serve You all the days of my life. I believe that Jesus Christ died on the cross for my sins.

Thank you so much for loving me, and waiting on me to come to the knowledge of the truth! Thank you for my salvation. Please help me and guide me in learning your Word so I can be a light to the world.

Please, Jesus, come into my heart and baptize me with your Holy Spirit. I thank You and praise Your Holy Name and ask all this in the name of Jesus Christ our Lord. Amen.

Sandra Lott was born and raised in San Antonio, Texas, with one sister and two brothers. Sandra loves the mountains, making candles, and jewelry. She is the author of Jeremy's Journey, Deep Waters Within, A Princess in Waiting, Ride the Wind, and more. She has also written children's such as, The Wind Has a Voice and How Did He Get in There, Molly's Journey to Forgiveness, and more. She has written over 34 books to date and began writing poetry as soon as she was saved in June 1998. The Lord gave her, her first book to write right after her son was killed. Writing was not something she sought out. She poured her heart into time spent with the Lord in order to allow Him to heal her heart and the name of her first book was birthed in her spirit along with the chapters and what it was to be about during a devotion time. It was called: God's Love; ironically enough, with all that she was going through, God's love was exactly what she needed.

She is passionate about studying the Bible. She has taught Sunday school, and Bible Study Groups, and has been actively serving in her present church, served in the Celebrate Recovery Ministry, and Homeless Outreach. Sandra was also interviewed on radio shows such as Golden Life Living and WMAP Radio (World's Most Amazing People based out of New York), the Bill Martinez show and a Fox Radio show called the Kim Kennedy Show.

She is a devoted mother of 2 sons (Tim & Gerald Ray), Gerald Ray the youngest, has gone on to be with the Lord due to a car accident. Through the death of her youngest son at the age of 16, a rocky marriage to an alcoholic and the abuse that came with that, and other overwhelming trials, she has drawn close to the loving arms of the Father. Experiencing God's unconditional love as He held her heart in His hands, has created a passion in her to help others grow in their understanding of and receive God's love and grow spiritually. She has the heart to help hurting women discover the princess in Christ that they truly are and overcome abuse. She teaches on topics to help you reach spiritual maturity, persevere through the hard times, and how to reach your destiny in Christ!

www.ingramcontent.com/pod-product-compliance
Lightning Source LLC
Chambersburg PA
CBHW051351150726
48000CB00003B/1134